Turnip is Missing

by Alison Hawes

Illustrated by Bill Ledger

OXFORD

UNIVERSITY PRESS

In this story ...

Ben

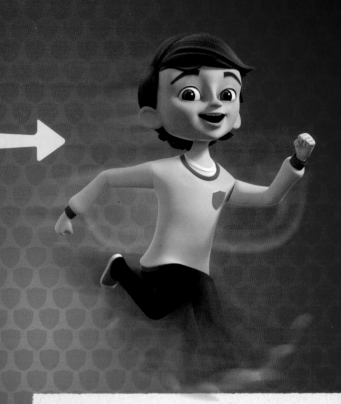

Ben can run fast. He is as fast as lightning.

Magnus

Turnip
(pet rat)

Ben is looking at a book.
Magnus bursts in.

My pet rat, Turnip, is missing!

Ben darts from the room.

I will look for Turnip.

Thank you.

Ben looks for Turnip but he cannot see him.

Ben spots Turnip in the garden.

Ben scoops Turnip up!

Ben hands Turnip to Magnus.

Magnus picks the thorns from Turnip's fur.

Retell the story ...

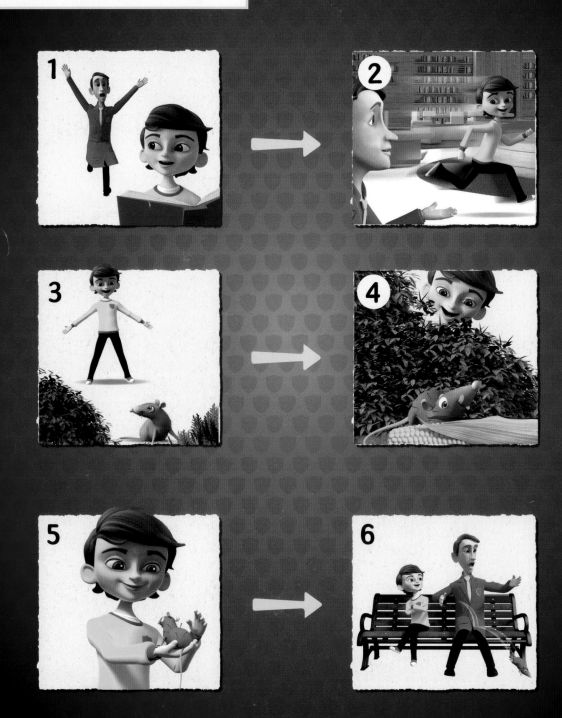